A DORLING KINDERSLEY BOOK

Editor Mary Ling
Designer Claire Penny
Managing Editor Sheila Hanly
Production Josie Alabaster
Photography Richard Leeney
Illustrator Ellis Nadler
Picture research Ingrid Nilsson

First published in Great Britain in 1996
by Dorling Kindersley Limited,
9 Henrietta Street, London WC2E 8PS

Copyright © 1996 Dorling Kindersley Limited

All rights reserved. No part of this publication may be reproduced, stored in a retrieval system, or transmitted in any form or by any means, electronic, mechanical, photocopying, recording or otherwise, without the prior written permission of the copyright owner.

A CIP catalogue record for this book is available from the British Library.

ISBN: 0-7513-5384-1

Colour reproduction by Chromagraphics, Singapore
Printed and bound in Italy by L.E.G.O.

Dorling Kindersley would like to thank: Ainscough Crane Hire Ltd, Lancs; British Aerospace Airbus Ltd, Chester; Halls Automotive, Kent; Redland Readymix, Darlington; WSM, Bristol for allowing their vehicles to be photographed and for all their help and advice.

The publisher would like to thank the following for their kind permission to reproduce their photographs:
l left, r right, t top, c centre b below
C Bingham 19tr; Robert Harding Picture Library 5br, 18/19c; Image Bank 8; Syndicated Truck Features/ Steve Sturgess 4/5c, 6/7bl; Telegraph Colour Library/ Masterfile 4bc, 9tr; S Windsor 9bl.

Every effort has been made to trace the copyright holders and we apologize in advance for any unintentional omissions. We would be pleased to insert the appropriate acknowledgement in any subsequent edition of this publication.

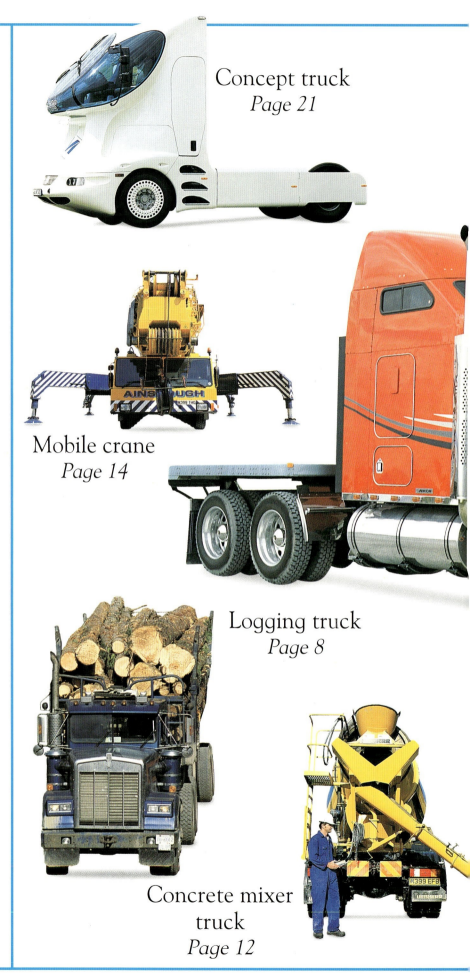

Concept truck
Page 21

Mobile crane
Page 14

Logging truck
Page 8

Concrete mixer truck
Page 12

Mighty Machines
Big Rig

Caroline Bingham

Heavy recovery truck
Page 16

Articulated truck
Page 6

Road train
Page 18

Oversize load
Page 10

DK

DORLING KINDERSLEY
LONDON · NEW YORK · STUTTGART

Articulated truck

An articulated truck, or rig, has an engine that is four times more powerful than any family-sized car's! It needs this power to pull heavy loads on long journeys. The truck has two sections – a tractor unit and a trailer, which can be separated from the tractor unit.

sleeping cabin

the front of a trailer links up to the tractor unit here

fuel to power the engine is stored in huge tanks

steps to driver's cab

The **tractor unit** contains the driver's cab, the front driving wheels, and the engine.

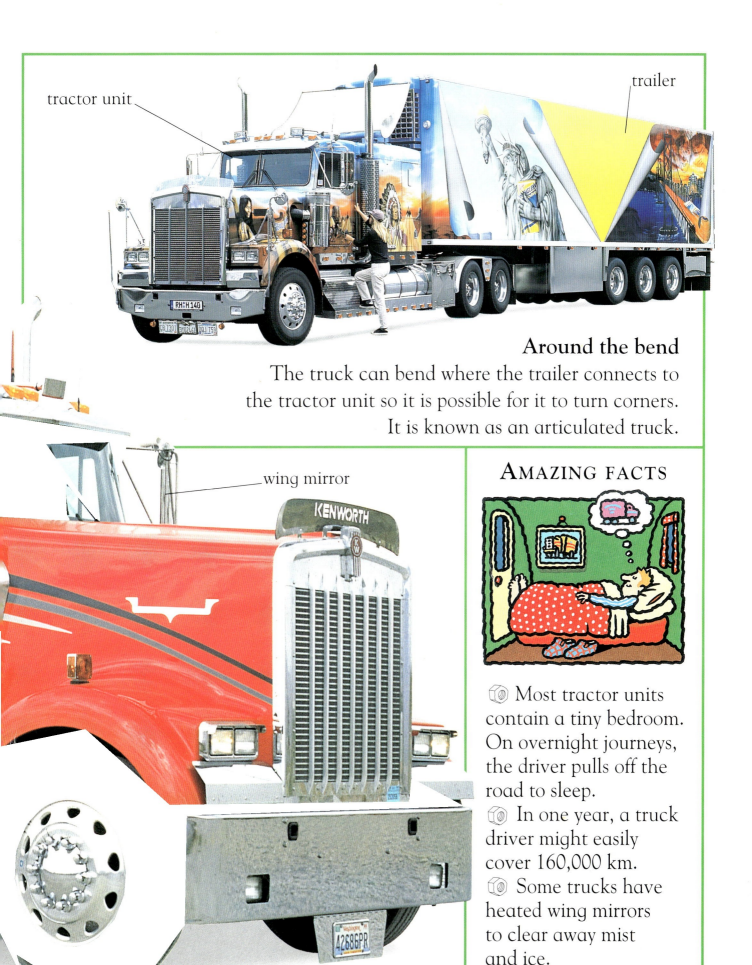

tractor unit

trailer

Around the bend
The truck can bend where the trailer connects to the tractor unit so it is possible for it to turn corners. It is known as an articulated truck.

wing mirror

AMAZING FACTS

- Most tractor units contain a tiny bedroom. On overnight journeys, the driver pulls off the road to sleep.
- In one year, a truck driver might easily cover 160,000 km.
- Some trucks have heated wing mirrors to clear away mist and ice.

A fully loaded articulated truck is often called a **rig**. **Trailers** carry goods.

Logging truck

A logging truck loads up with huge tree trunks at a tree-felling site and takes them to a sawmill. The trunks are held in place on the open trailer by metal rods and are secured with cables.

branches are sawn off the tree trunk before it is transported

logs are piled high behind the driver's cab

metal rod

Trees are cut down at **tree-felling sites**.

Grab and hold

Some logging trucks have built-in cranes and can load themselves, but often a separate crane machine puts the logs in place. The crane grips the logs – just like you would pick up a handful of pencils.

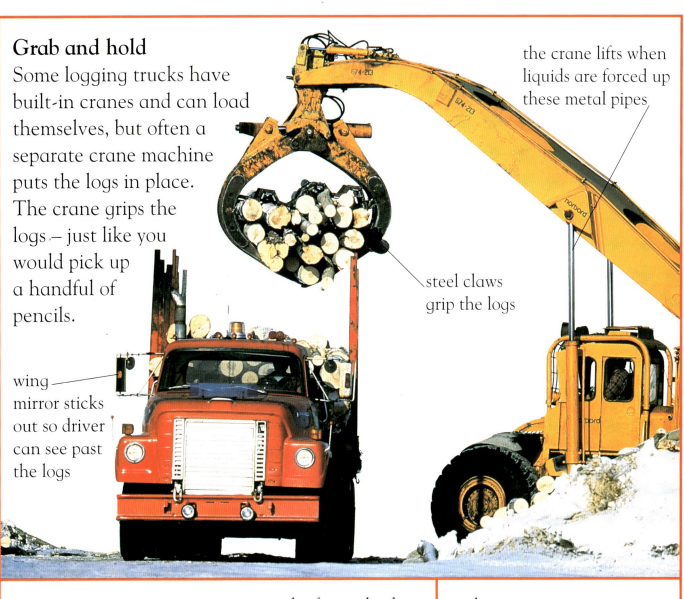

the crane lifts when liquids are forced up these metal pipes

steel claws grip the logs

wing mirror sticks out so driver can see past the logs

the engine is protected by a bonnet

the front wheels are covered by a wheel arch

all trucks have loud air horns

Amazing Facts

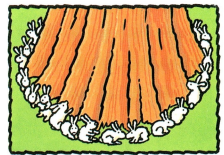

 If a logging truck carried one huge tree, the tree's base would be big enough for 40 bunnies to hop around nose to tail.

 Logs are stripped of bark and cut up at **sawmills**. A **bonnet** covers a truck's engine.

Oversize load

Trucks sometimes have to carry oddly-shaped loads. They might need to transport a boat, or even a house! This truck is carrying a wing for a passenger plane. The loaded truck is very heavy and long, and the driver has to travel slowly. On public roads, a truck with an oversize load often has a police escort.

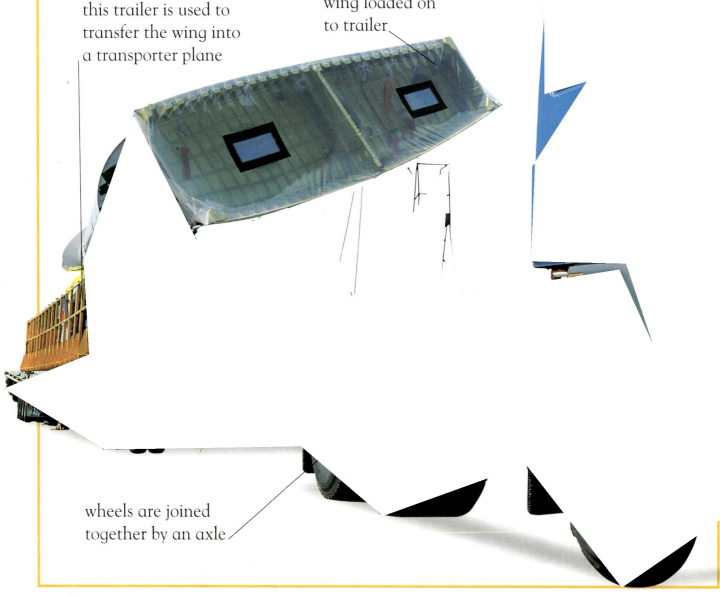

this trailer is used to transfer the wing into a transporter plane

wing loaded on to trailer

wheels are joined together by an axle

An **axle** is a metal rod that joins a set of wheels. **Reverse** means go backwards.

Remote control steering

The back of the trailer is steered around corners by remote control.

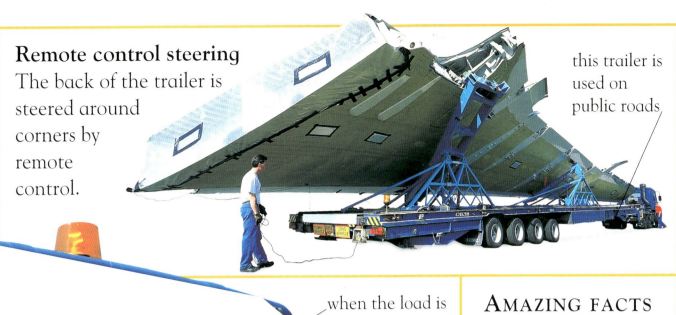

this trailer is used on public roads

when the load is secure, the driver will reverse to hitch the tractor unit to the trailer

a bumper helps to protect the truck if it is involved in an accident

Amazing facts

🔩 This wing is as heavy as 525 seven-year-old children. But this many children would take up a lot more space.

🔩 The loaded wing will squeeze under motorway bridges leaving a gap little bigger than the length of a banana. That's a tight fit!

🔩 When the wing is on the trailer on a public road, the rig is 38 m long. That's as long as 12 elephants linked up trunk to tail.

Remote control gives an operator control from a distance.

Concrete mixer truck

AMAZING FACTS

🔩 A concrete mixer spins its load like a giant washing machine – in fact, it could wash 100 loads at once.

🔩 The blades inside the mixer's drum force the watery concrete uphill.

🔩 Six tonnes of sand are used to load a mixer truck. That's enough to build a two metre high sandcastle.

🔩 A concrete mixer is unstable because of the concrete sloshing around the drum.

Spot a concrete mixer truck on the road and you will see the drum turning round and round. It turns to mix its load and keep it from setting before the truck finishes its journey at a building site.

cab-over tractor unit

🔩 In **cab-over** trucks the driver sits above the engine and front wheels.

Which way? The drum turns one way to mix the concrete and the other way to empty it.

ready-mixed concrete leaves the drum along this chute

driver empties drum by remote control

drum

the driver climbs the ladder to check the load

Concrete is a mixture of sand, gravel, cement, and water.

Mobile crane

AMAZING FACTS

Four huge metal legs called outriggers stretch out and then their feet find a firm position on the ground. The long arm, or jib, begins to reach up into the air and the mobile crane is ready to lift its load.

Front view

feet, or jacks

outrigger

- This crane can lift 500 tonnes – that's the same weight as 500 family cars.

- The crane has two engines – one to drive the vehicle and one to operate the jib.

- The crane's 18 wheels are all connected to the steering. When the crane turns, the back wheels turn at a different angle to the front wheels.

- When the jib is lifting, a counterweight is attached. It's as heavy as the crane itself.

A **counterweight** is a heavy metal weight. It stops the crane from tipping over.

Fold up and go

Mobile cranes work on building and road construction sites, lifting heavy objects. When the operator wants to drive the crane to a new site, the jib pulls in on itself like a telescope.

the jib telescopes out from here

hook block is attached to cab when the crane is on the road

The **jib** is a long metal arm.　**Jacks** are big metal feet used to steady a machine.　15

Heavy recovery truck

With its bright colours and flashing lights, this recovery truck is easy to spot as it approaches the scene of an accident. Once there, it slides a long piece of steel called an underlift under the damaged vehicle, or casualty, and tows it to a garage to be repaired.

a heat shield surrounds the exhaust pipe

sleeping cabin

underlift

tools are stored in this locker

this truck has 62 sidelights

the engine runs on diesel fuel, stored in two huge tanks

16 The recovery truck's operator calls a damaged vehicle a **casualty**.

Using spectacles

This recovery truck has hooked a metal frame, or spectacle lift, under the front wheels of a casualty.

spectacles

emergency lights flash to warn people to keep clear of the truck

two side markers help the driver to judge the width of the truck

ballast bumper

Amazing facts

🔩 The ballast bumper weighs 1.5 tonnes. That's as heavy as 11 baby elephants.

🔩 This truck can pull more than five times its own weight. Could you pull five of your friends?

🔩 **Ballast** acts as a counterweight when the truck is towing a heavy vehicle.

Road train

A road train pulls three or four trailers in the same way that a train pulls carriages, but it doesn't need track, it travels on the road. In Australia, the distances between some cities are so vast that long road trains are the best way to transport goods.

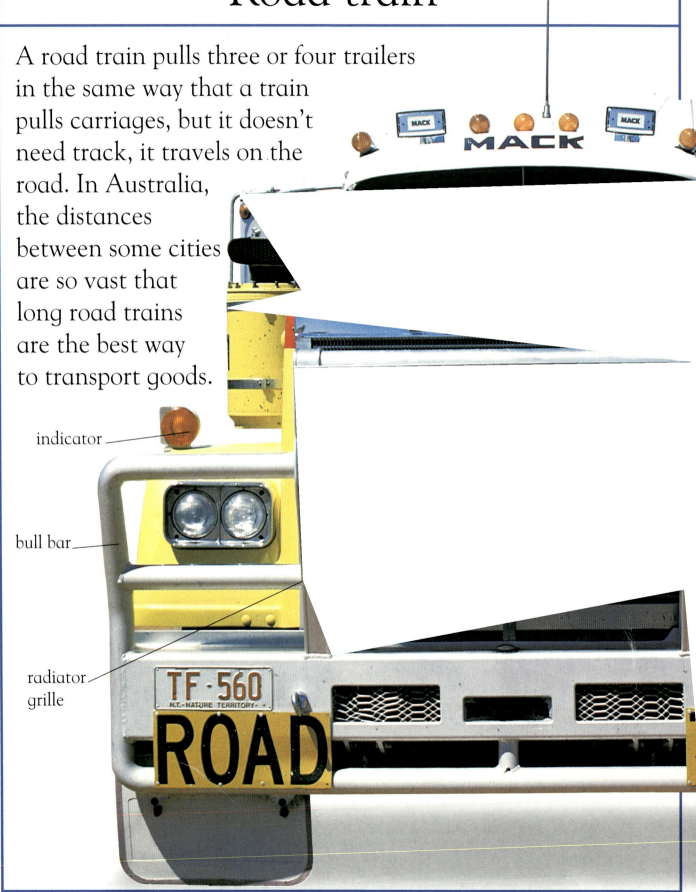

indicator

bull bar

radiator grille

Indicators flash orange when the driver turns a corner or pulls over.

It bends like a snake

This road train is transporting fuel. Three trailers are hitched together so the train can bend.

exhaust pipe

trailer containing fuel

bug deflector helps keep the windscreen clear of insects

air is sucked in and cleaned in this barrel. It mixes with the fuel to make the engine go

No entry

A road train cannot enter a city – it's too big! So the driver loads and unloads at special road train stations. A road train carries enough fuel to travel 3,520 km.

road trains are marked so other drivers know the vehicle is unusually long

Amazing facts

🔩 The most powerful road train has the pulling power of 600 strong horses.

🔩 You would have to link up with 414 friends to make a chain the length of the longest road train in the world (379 m).

 Waste fumes leave the engine through the **exhaust pipe**.

Supertruck

A big rig has to push through lots of air as it roars along a road. If a designer can cut down on air resistance, or drag, the truck will save fuel because the engine won't have to work as hard to drive the rig along. The best way to do this is to make the truck a smoother shape – like this sleek, new supertruck.

collar forces air up and over the back of the trailer

panels cover wheels to provide a smooth surface for air to flow over

Aerodynamic shapes often have rounded edges to help them slip through the air.

Concept truck

In trying to make trucks more aerodynamic in order to save fuel, truck designers sometimes develop ideas which look unusual. Just look at the shape of this truck!

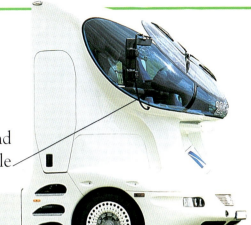

driver sits behind a glass bubble

AMAZING FACTS

🔩 Compared to older rigs, the supertruck saves about 50 drink cans' worth of fuel every 100 km. It would take a long time to get through that much fizzy drink.

🔩 The supertruck has only 12 wheels. Older trucks of this size may have 22 wheels.

🔩 The supertruck's cab is so tall that an adult can comfortably stand up inside it.

A **concept truck** is a truck which tries out a designer's new ideas.